The Step-by-Step Way to Draw Motorcycle

A Fun and Easy Drawing Book to Learn How to Draw Motorcycles

By

Kristen Diaz.

Copyright 2019 Kristen Diaz.

License Notes

No part of this Book can be reproduced in any form or by any means including print, electronic, scanning or photocopying unless prior permission is granted by the author.

All ideas, suggestions and guidelines mentioned here are written for informative purposes. While the author has taken every possible step to ensure accuracy, all readers are advised to follow information at their own risk. The author cannot be held responsible for personal and/or commercial damages in case of misinterpreting and misunderstanding any part of this Book

Table of Contents

Introduction 4

How to draw a chopper 5

How to draw a Honda motorcycle 25

How to draw a Kawasaki motorcycle 45

About the Author 65

Introduction

Becoming a great artist requires creativity, patience and practice. These habits can flourish in children when they start to develop them at a young age. We believe our guide will teach your child the discipline and patience required to not just learn to draw well, but to use those qualities in everything they do. Your job as a parent is to work with your child and encourage them when stuck and feel like giving up.

The world of art is an amazing way for you and your child to communicate and bond. When you open this book and start to create with your little one, you will delight in the things you learn about them and they will feel closer to you. Your support and gentle suggestions will help them be more patient with themselves and soon they will take the time needed to create spectacular drawings of which you can both be proud.

This guide is useful for parents as it teaches fundamentals of drawing and simple techniques. By following this book with your child, adults will learn patience and develop their skills as a child's most important teacher. By spending a few hours together you will develop a strong connection and learn the best ways of communicating with each other. It is truly a rewarding experience when you and your child create a masterpiece by working together!

How to draw a chopper

Step 1

Draw a rectangle for the steering stem and a big shape for the body of the bike, and the head light.

How to draw a chopper

Step 1

Draw a rectangle for the steering stem and a big shape for the body of the bike, and the head light.

Step 2

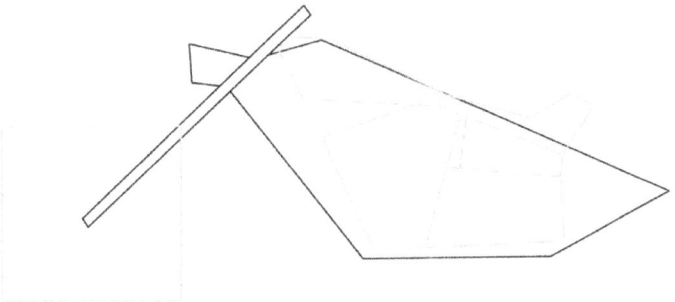

Add a square for the outline of the front wheel.

Then add the outline for the saddle and the different sections inside the bike.

Step 3

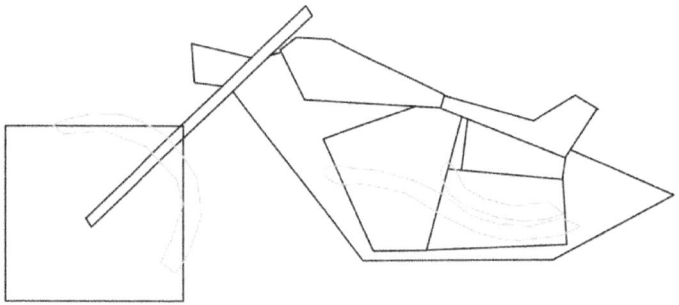

Add the outline of the front wheel cover and the exhaust pipes.

Step 4

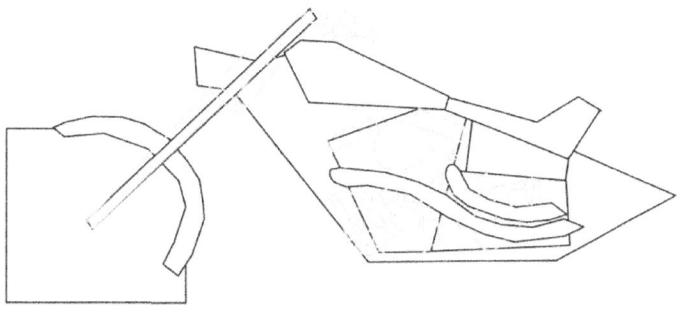

Redraw the outline of the steering stem to add some detail to it, including the outline of the fork and the handlebars to steer with. Then add the basic shapes for the engine parts as in the example.

Step 5

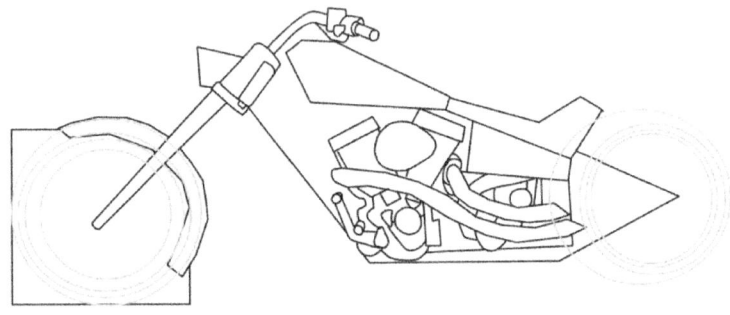

Add the outline for the front and the rear wheel.

Step 6.

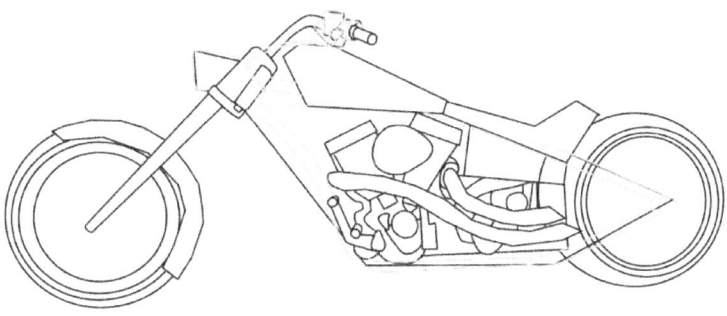

Go back up to the steering part of the bike. Add the different part of the steering stem. Redraw the headlight to smooth it out, then add the braking cable down the stem. Add the side of the fork to make the handlebars. Add small appendixes to show where the rearview mirrors are.

Add the handle bar and other small details as shown in the example. Then draw the frame around the bike as in the example.

Step 7

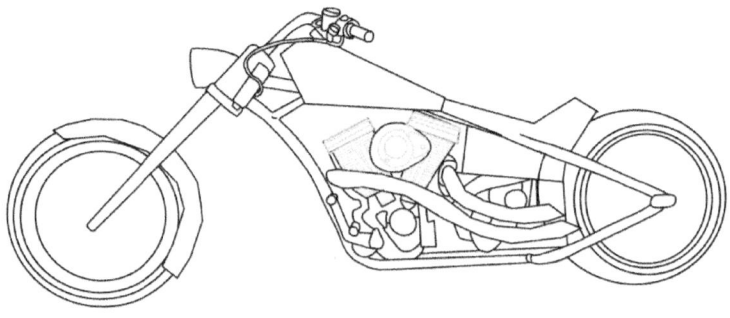

Continue to the engine. Redraw the top part of the engine as in the example.

Step 8

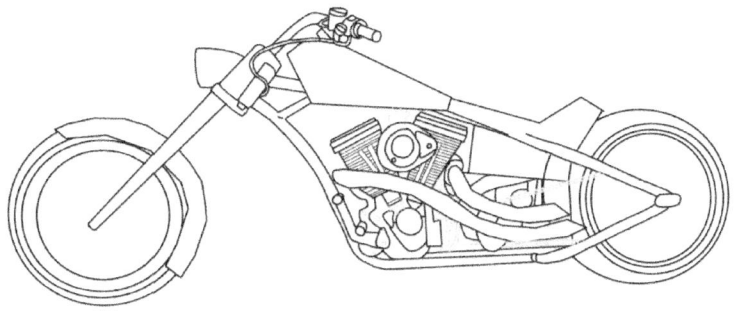

Pay close attention to the example.

Follow along to add the different parts of the engine block and add the chain to regulate the gears used while driving.

Step 9

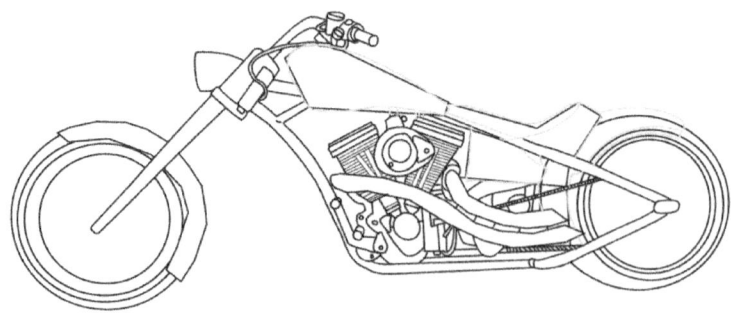

Smooth out the fuel tank by redrawing it.

Add the seat of the saddle and then continue the upper body frame to the rear cover.

Step 10

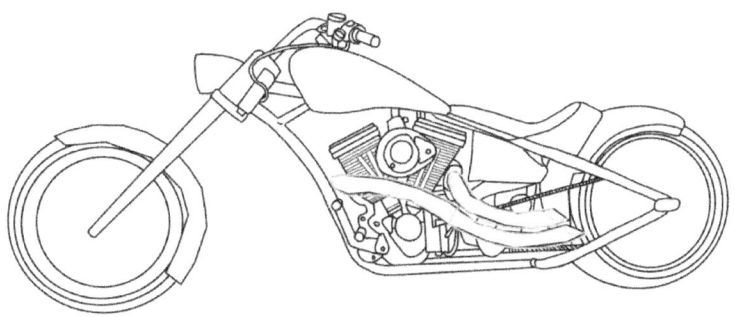

Redraw the exhaust pipes to smooth them out.

Step 11

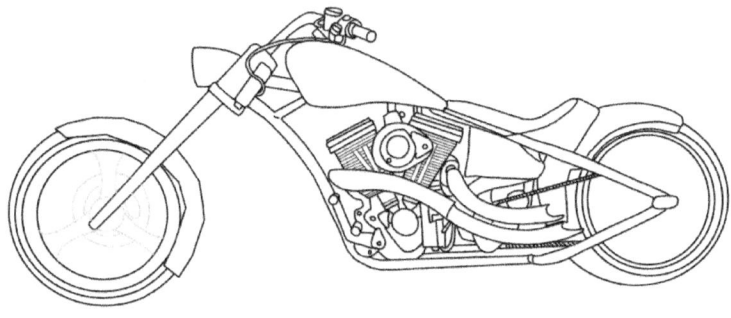

Add the outline of the front breaks around the steering stem.
Then add the rims as in the example.

Step 12

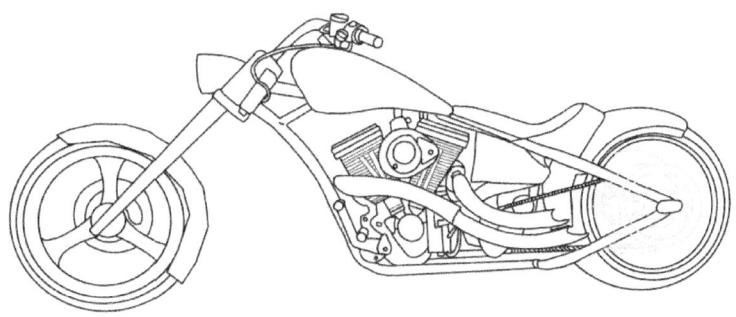

Add the outline of the rear brakes and the mechanism regulating the chain to shift gear.

Add the ring around the rear brake and the rear brake itself.

Connect the chain to the rear wheel as in the example.

Step 13

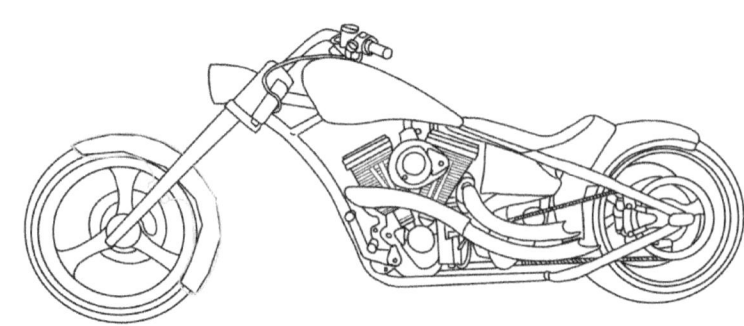

Redraw the front cover over the front wheel as in the example.

Step 14

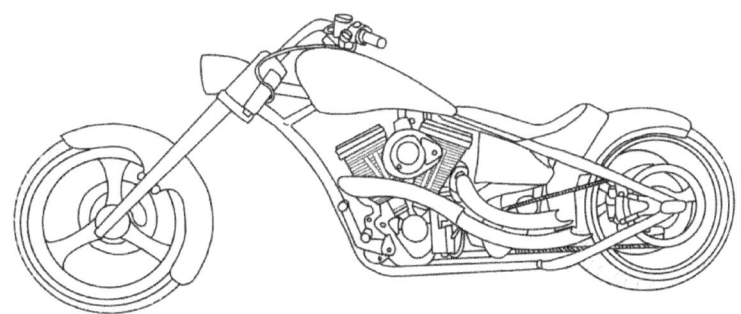

Add the lines inside the wheels for traction.

Step 15

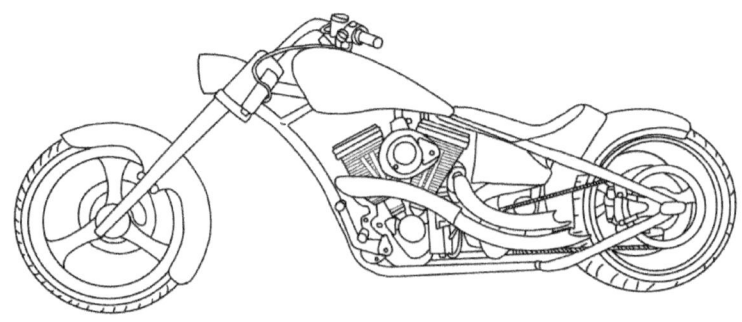

All done! Let's color!

Step 16

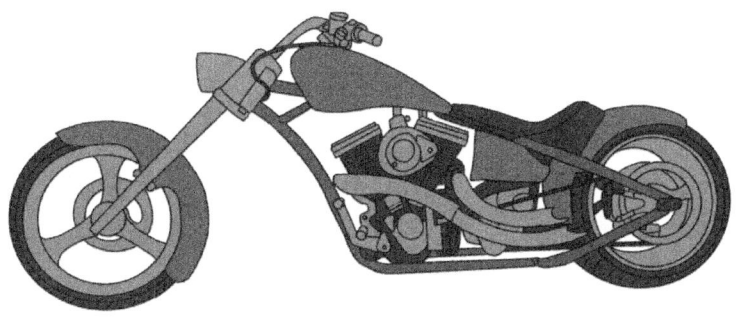

The fuel tank, the covers and the body of the bike are purple. The engine, front wheel frame, the steering stem, the fork and the handlebars are grey. The exhaust pipes are grey. The seat is dark grey.

Step 17

Add shadow and highlights to pimp out motorcycle out.

Step 18

Colored version.

Step 19

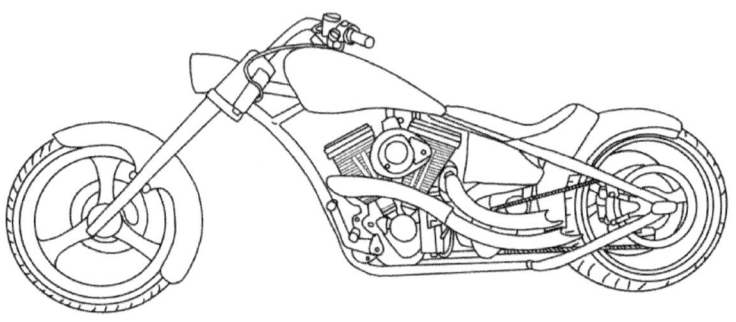

Line art version.

How to draw a Honda motorcycle

Step 1

Draw a rectangle for the steering stem and a big shape for the body of the bike.

Step 2

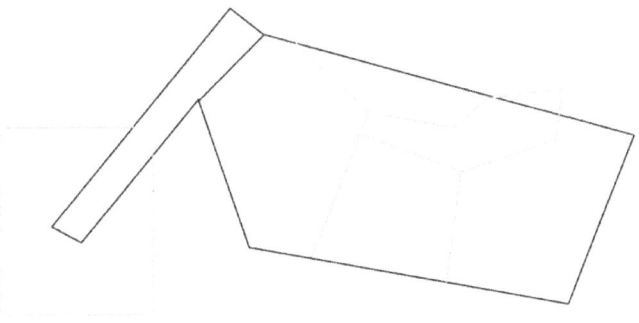

Add a square for the outline of the front wheel.

Then add the outline for the saddle and the different sections inside the bike.

Step 3

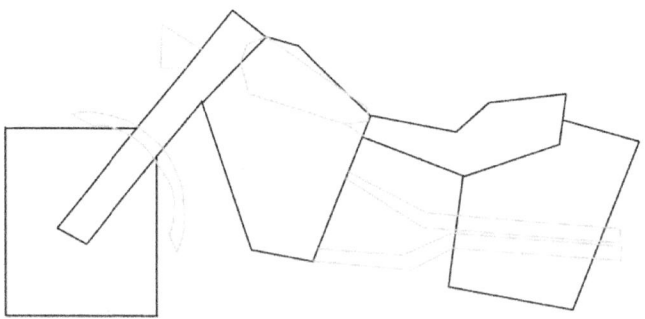

Add the outline of the front wheel cover.

Then the outline for the fuel tank, the headlight, and the exhaust pipes.

Step 4

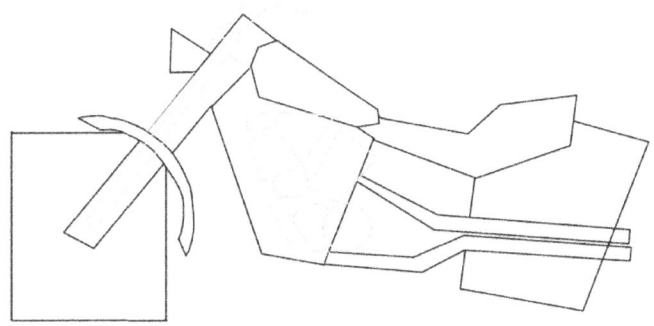

Redraw the outline of the steering stem to add some detail to it, including the outline of the fork to steer with. Then add the basic shapes for the engine parts as in the example.

Step 5

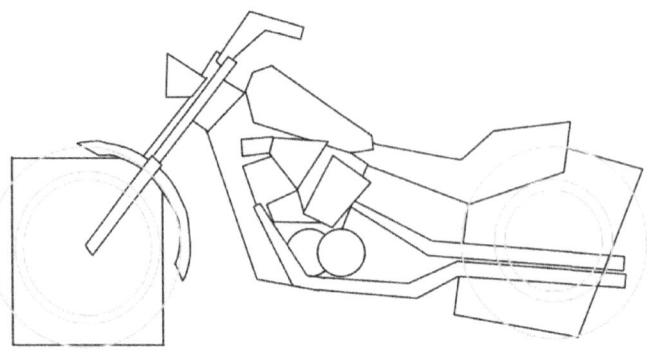

Add the outline for the front and the rear wheel.

Step 6

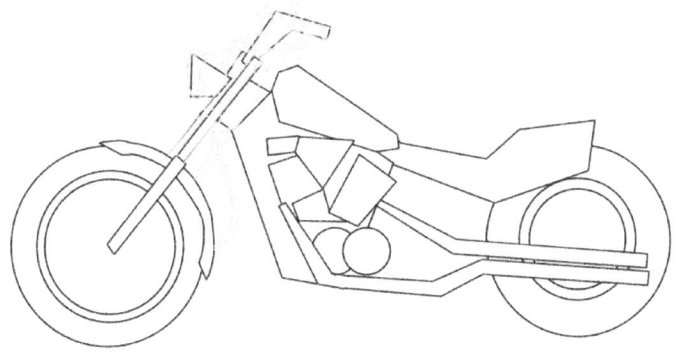

Go back up to the steering part of the bike. Add the different part of the steering stem. Redraw the headlight to smooth it out. Add the breaking cables leading up to the steering fork, then redraw the side of the fork to make the handlebars. Add small appendixes to show where the rearview mirrors are. Add the handle bar and other small details as shown in the example.

Step 7

Continue to the engine. Add the front radiator to the front section of the engine block. Make sure to add the slanted lines to show where the air is sucked in.

Step 8

Pay close attention to the example.

Follow along to add the different parts of the engine block. Add the connector for the exhaust pipes.

Step 9

Smooth out the fuel tank by redrawing it.

Add the seat of the saddle and then continue the upper body frame to the rear cover and the brake light.

Step 10

Redraw the exhaust pipes to smooth them out.

Then add the final parts and details to the inner part of the engine. Lastly, add the standard underneath the body.

Step 11

Add the inner lines of the front wheel.

Then add the outline of the front breaks around the steering stem.

Step 12

Now add the inner lines for the rear wheel.

Include some final details to the rear part of the engine. Then add the outline of the rear brakes and the spring connecting it to the bike.

Step 13

Add the rims to the inside of the wheels.

38

Step 14

Add the lines inside the wheels for traction.

Step 15

All done! Let's color!

Step 16

The fuel tank, the covers and the body of the bike are orange. The engine, the exhaust pipes and the engine block are grey. The frame of the bikes is very dark blue. The seat is dark grey.

Step 17

Add shadow and highlights to pimp out motorcycle out.

Step 18

Colored version.

Step 19

Line art version.

How to draw a Kawasaki motorcycle

Step 1

Draw a rectangle for the steering stem and a big shape for the body of the bike.

Step 2

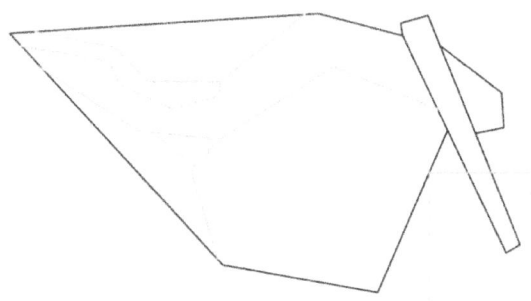

Add a square for the outline of the front wheel.

Then add the outline for the saddle and the different sections inside the bike.

Step 3

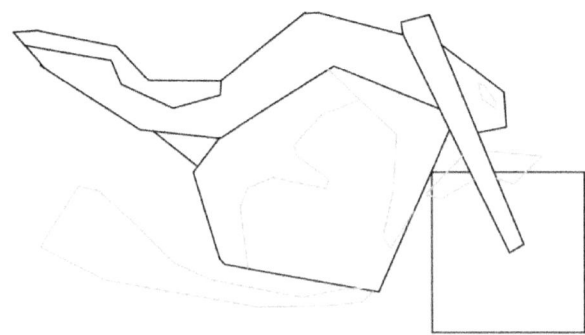

Add the outline of the front wheel cover.

Then the outline for the headlight, and the exhaust pipes.

Step 4

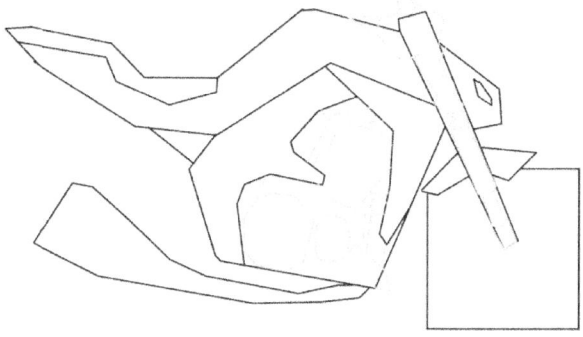

Redraw the outline of the steering stem to add some detail to it, including the outline of the fork to steer with. Then add the basic shapes for the engine parts as in the example.

Step 5

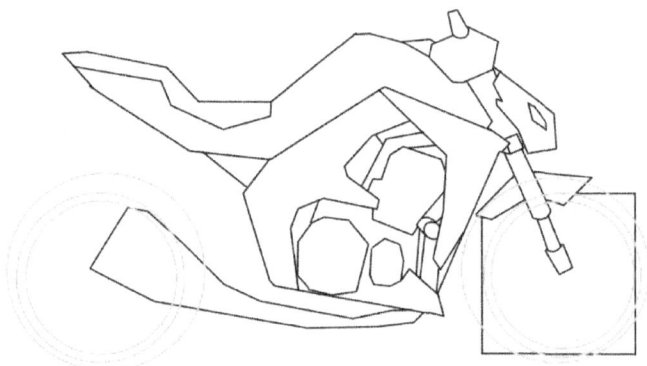

Add the outline for the front and the rear wheel.

Step 6

Go back up to the steering part of the bike. Add the different part of the steering stem. Redraw the headlight to smooth it out. Add the side of the fork to make the handlebars. Add small appendixes to show where the rearview mirrors are. Add the handle bar and other small details as shown in the example.

Step 7

Continue to the engine. Add the top part of the plates that cover the majority of the engine.

Step 8

Pay close attention to the example. Follow along to add the different parts of the engine block.

Step 9

Smooth out the fuel tank by redrawing it.

Add the seat of the saddle and then continue the upper body frame to the rear cover and the brake light. Pay close attention to the shape of the body. See how almost futuristically reptilian it looks like? Then add the rear part of the cover covering the majority of the engine.

Step 10

Redraw the exhaust pipes to smooth them out.

Then add the final parts and details to the rear part of the engine. Pay close attention to the example to make sure your detail is just as great!

Step 11

Add the outline of the front breaks around the steering stem. Add the braking cable leading up to the bike. Add the metal parts around the front breaks.

Step 12

Add the outline of the rear brakes and the mechanism regulating the chain to shift gear.

Step 13

Add the rims to the inside of the wheels.

Pay close attention to see how to draw them.

Step 14

Add the lines inside the wheels for traction.

Step 15

All done! Let's color!

Step 16

The fuel tank, the covers and the body of the bike are green. The engine, front wheel frame, the steering stem, the fork and the handlebars are dark grey. The exhaust pipes are dark blue, with light grey at the end. The front part of the cooling tubes are dark brown. The seat is dark blue and the braking light is red.

Step 17

Add shadow and highlights to pimp out motorcycle out.

Step 18

Colored version.

Step 19

Line art version.

About the Author

Kristen Diaz is an accomplished artist and e-book author living in Southern California. She has provided the illustrations for hundreds of children's books as her realistic and lifelike images appeal to children and adults alike.

Diaz began her career as an artist when she was in her 20's creating caricatures on the beaches of sunny California. What started as a way to make extra spending money turned into a successful career because of her amazing talent. Her comically accurate caricatures had a unique look and one of the local authors took notice. When the writer asked Diaz to illustrate one of her books, Kristen jumped at the opportunity to showcase her talent. The result was spectacular and soon Diaz was in high demand. Her ability to change her style to fit the books made her an attractive artist to work with.

She decided to get a more formal education in graphic design and illustration by enrolling in the Arts program at Platt's College which is where she met the love of her life and life partner, Terri. The two live in Pasadena close to the beach where Diaz' career first flourished. She occasionally hangs out on the beach with her easel and paints and makes caricatures of the humanity passing by. Her e-books are simple to follow and contain many witty anecdotes about her life in Pasadena.

Printed in Great Britain
by Amazon